THE BATTLE OF GETTYSBURG

THE BATTLE OF
GETTYSBURG
ALDEN R. CARTER

Franklin Watts
New York / London / Toronto / Sydney
A First Book 1990

For Bill, Joan, Matthew,
and Isabelle

Many thanks to all who helped
with The Battle of Gettysburg,
particularly my editor, Reni Roxas;
my mother, Hilda Carter Fletcher;
and my friends Don Beyer, Barbara
Feinberg, and Dean Markwardt.
As always, my wife, Carol,
deserves much of the credit.

Maps by Joe LeMonnier

Diagram by Vantage Art

Cover painting courtesy of: State Museum of Pennsylvania

Photographs courtesy of: Snite Museum of Art: p. 2; Historical Picture Service:
pp. 9, 58 (top right); New York Picture Library: pp. 10, 32 (top & bottom),
57, 58 (top left, all bottom), 59 (all top, bottom left & center); The Bettmann
Archive: pp. 12, 19, 22, 26, 54, 55, 58 (top center), 59 (bottom right);
Smithsonian Institute: p. 32 (center); State Museum of Pennsylvania: p. 41;
Wadsworth Atheneum: p. 42; Carol S. Carter: pp. 61 (both).

Library of Congress Cataloging-in-Publication Data
Carter, Alden R.
The Battle of Gettysburg / Alden R. Carter.
p.   cm. — (A First book)
Includes bibliographical references (p.   ).
Summary: Describes the Confederate Army's northern campaign, its
defeat at the Battle of Gettysburg, and the subsequent effect on the
course of the Civil War.
ISBN 0-531-10852-X
1. Gettysburg, Battle of, 1863—Juvenile literature.
[1. Gettysburg, Battle of, 1863.   2. United States—History—Civil
War. 1861–1865—Campaigns.]   I. Title.   II. Series.
E475.53.C28   1990
973.7'349—dc20   89-37033   CIP   AC

CONTENTS

Officers Listed in the Text

CONFEDERATE:
The Army of
    Northern Virginia

Gen. Robert E. Lee,
    commanding

Lt. Gen. Richard Ewell
Lt. Gen. Ambrose Hill
Lt. Gen. James Longstreet

Maj. Gen. Richard Anderson
Maj. Gen. Jubal Early
Maj. Gen. Henry Heth
Maj. Gen. John Hood
Maj. Gen. Lafayette McLaws
Maj. Gen. George Pickett
Maj. Gen. Robert Rodes
Maj. Gen. J.E.B. Stuart

Brig. Gen. Lewis Armistead
Brig. Gen. William Barksdale
Brig. Gen. James Pettigrew

Col. E. Porter Alexander
Col. William Oates

UNION:
The Army of the
    Potomac

Maj. Gen. George Meade,
    commanding

Maj. Gen. Joseph Hooker,
    previous commander
Maj. Gen. Abner Doubleday
Maj. Gen. Winfield Hancock
Maj. Gen. Oliver Howard
Maj. Gen. John Reynolds
Maj. Gen. John Sedgwick
Maj. Gen. Daniel Sickles

Brig. Gen. John Buford
Brig. Gen. Henry Hunt
Brig. Gen. Gouverneur Warren

Col. Arthur Devereux

Lt. Alonzo Cushing

Maj. Gen Ulysses S. Grant,
    commanding Union
    army at Vicksburg

1

THE ROAD NORTH

The Confederate Army of Northern Virginia needed shoes. It also needed pants, coats, blankets, bacon, flour, coffee, sugar, medicine, gunpowder, bullets, horses, wagons, cattle, and scores of other things. It even needed sauerkraut, thought to be a remedy for the diarrhea that plagued thousands of soldiers. In fact, it seemed that the Army of Northern Virginia needed just about everything. But, most of all, it needed a great victory.

General Robert E. Lee knew this. His lean, ragged, often barefoot men had fought with a courage and endurance far beyond what any general could expect. They were, he felt sure, the best soldiers ever to serve in an army. But even they could not fight forever without enough supplies.

In this late spring of 1863, the American Civil War was entering its third year. Eleven Southern states were fighting for the right to found their own country—the Confederate States of America. But the United States government argued that no such right existed; the union of *all* the states was sacred and could not be broken. Tens of thousands of Northern soldiers just as brave as Lee's Confederates were determined to fight—and if necessary die—to save the Union.

So far, most of the major battles had been fought in Maryland and northern Virginia. Time and again, the Army of Northern Virginia had whipped the larger and better equipped Union Army of the Potomac. Yet, all the victories had not won the war, and Lee knew that time was running short.

The North had many factories and a large population; the agricultural South lacked both. Northern factories could turn out five thousand rifles a day, Southern workshops only a hundred. Union troops ate well and got new blue uniforms when their old ones wore thin. Confederate troops ate poorly, and few now wore the uniform gray of the early months of the war. Instead, they dressed in a hodgepodge of rough clothing dyed a butternut tan. Most important, the Union army could replace its losses easily with new recruits, while Lee saw his army bleeding to death with every battle.

With a larger population and more factories, the North could afford a longer war than the South. In this Northern factory, women are making munitions for the Union Army of the Potomac.

Major General Ulysses S. Grant, commander of the Union army hammering at the gates of the Confederate stronghold of Vicksburg, Mississippi. In 1864, Lincoln would give him command of all the Union armies.

Outside Virginia, the war was going poorly for the South. The Union navy patrolled the coast, cutting off supplies from overseas. In the West, a powerful Union army under General Ulysses S. Grant hammered at the Confederate stronghold of Vicksburg, Mississippi. If Vicksburg fell, the Union would control the Mississippi River, splitting the Confederacy in two.

The time had come for the South to risk everything for a great victory. In his headquarters at Fredericksburg, Virginia, on the south side of the Rappahannock River, Lee studied his maps. He would invade the North, marching across Maryland and into the rich farmland of Pennsylvania. There he would lure the Army of the Potomac into battle and destroy it once and for all. The important cities of Baltimore, Philadelphia, and Washington, the nation's capital, would lie at his mercy. Northerners opposed to the war would riot in the streets. Nations in Europe would recognize the Confederacy as an independent nation, perhaps even sending their warships to break the Union navy's stranglehold. Grant would have to rush troops east, leaving Vicksburg in Confederate hands. One great Confederate victory in Pennsylvania, and the United States government would beg for peace. The South would at last be free.

On June 3, 1863, Lee set his army on the road north. Few of his men doubted that Lee would lead them to victory. The soldiers adored their handsome, gray-haired general. He seemed everything that a Southern gentleman should be—polite, kind, brave, and unselfish.

Robert Edward Lee came from a well-known Virginia family with a long record of public service. He graduated from the United States Military Academy at West Point in 1829 and served with distinc-

General Robert E. Lee, commander of the Confederate Army of Northern Virginia. No general in the Civil War was so loved by his own men or so respected by his opponents.

tion in the army for more than thirty years. At the start of the Civil War in 1861, President Abraham Lincoln offered Lee command of the Army of the Potomac. Lee refused. He opposed slavery, the main issue leading to war, but he could not bring himself to fight against his native state. Sadly, he rode south to offer his services to the Confederacy.

Two years later, President Lincoln was still trying to find a satisfactory commander for the Army of the Potomac. In early June 1863, the Union army was camped on the north side of the Rappahannock. General Joseph "Fighting Joe" Hooker had 115,000 men to Lee's 70,000. Hooker's men were in good condition: well trained, well fed, and well equipped. Most were hardened veterans, as used to long marches and fierce fighting as Lee's. But "Fighting Joe" had shown no more talent for fighting than the army's three previous commanders.

Hooker soon had reports of long Confederate columns on the march. What was Lee planning? For days he tried to find out, but Lee concealed the movement of his infantry behind a screen of cavalry that turned back every probe by Union horsemen.

Finally convinced that Lee was heading north, Hooker sent his own plan to Washington. Instead of chasing Lee, he wanted to cross the Rappahannock and strike at the Confederate capital of Richmond,

Virginia. Lincoln said no, ordering Hooker to march north: "Lee's army, not Richmond is your true objective." Hooker sulked but obeyed. On June 13, the Army of the Potomac began moving slowly north.

By this time, the spearhead of Lee's army had swung wide of Hooker's army and was pushing steadily north toward the Potomac River. Lee's foot soldiers marched in three corps of about 20,000 men each. General Richard Ewell's Second Corps led the advance. One-legged "Baldy" Ewell was a brave and capable officer, but he felt unsure of himself in his new role as a corps commander.

Ewell's corps crossed the Blue Ridge Mountains and marched north along the Shenandoah Valley. Small, fierce fights raged to the east as Union cavalry tried unsuccessfully to punch through the Confederate screen. On June 14, Ewell's men reached Winchester, Virginia, where they captured nearly 4,000 Union troops with little trouble.

A day or two behind Ewell's corps came the battering ram of the army: General James "Old Pete" Longstreet's First Corps. At forty-two, Longstreet was an experienced and talented commander, and Lee relied heavily on his big, slow-spoken friend. Longstreet was worried; Lee seemed too anxious for battle, despite Longstreet's warnings about the dangers of fighting on Northern soil.

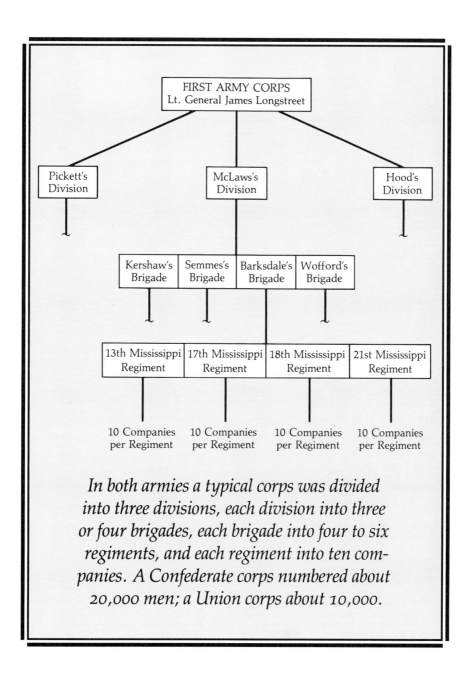

FIRST ARMY CORPS
Lt. General James Longstreet

Pickett's Division

McLaws's Division

Hood's Division

Kershaw's Brigade | Semmes's Brigade | Barksdale's Brigade | Wofford's Brigade

13th Mississippi Regiment | 17th Mississippi Regiment | 18th Mississippi Regiment | 21st Mississippi Regiment

10 Companies per Regiment | 10 Companies per Regiment | 10 Companies per Regiment | 10 Companies per Regiment

In both armies a typical corps was divided into three divisions, each division into three or four brigades, each brigade into four to six regiments, and each regiment into ten companies. A Confederate corps numbered about 20,000 men; a Union corps about 10,000.

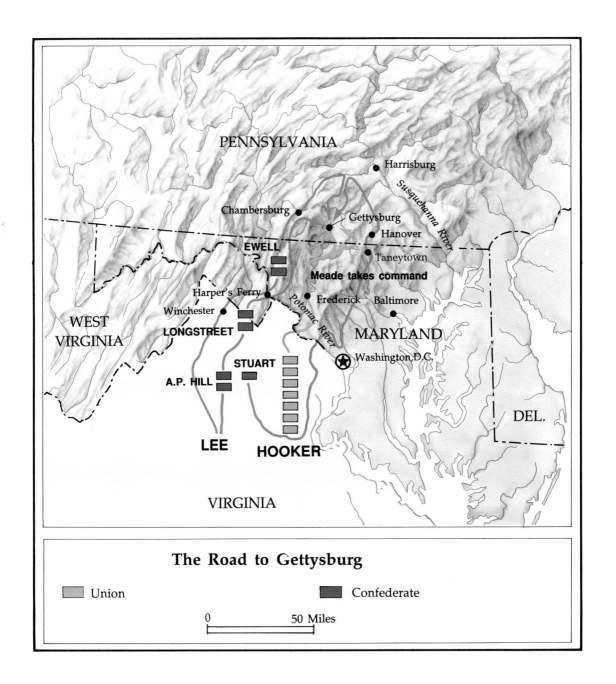

The Road to Gettysburg

Union

Confederate

0   50 Miles

As the rest of the infantry headed north, General Ambrose Powell Hill and his Third Corps waited near the Rappahannock, guarding against a Union move on Richmond. A. P. Hill was able, popular, and recklessly brave. Eager to preserve Third Corps's reputation for fast marching and hard striking, Hill waited impatiently for his turn to march.

An even more impatient man also longed for action. General J. E. B. "Jeb" Stuart, the youthful commander of Lee's cavalry, was nursing his wounded pride. On June 9, Union cavalry had surprised Stuart's men at Brandy Station, Virginia. For almost the first time in the war, the Union cavalry had fought with the courage and skill of the Confederates. After a fierce fight, Stuart's famed horsemen had finally driven them back across the Rappahannock. But the Union surprise had embarrassed Stuart, and he longed to teach the Northern cavalry a lesson.

The Army of the Potomac's move north freed both Hill and Stuart. Hill hurried his men across the Rappahannock, while Stuart's men screened the crossing. With the last of the infantry safely on the road north, Stuart was at last able to seek his revenge. He had orders from Lee to bring the cavalry north as soon as possible. The cavalry were the "eyes and ears" of the army, and Lee wanted them out in front as the army pushed across the Potomac into Maryland and enemy territory.

It was Lee's practice to give his commanders only general instructions, trusting them to work out the details. Stuart had a bold plan for regaining his reputation. Instead of taking a direct route to the Potomac, he would ride *around* the Union army, scaring the daylights out of the towns near Washington before circling back to join Ewell's corps north of the Potomac.

Just past midnight on June 25, Stuart led 5,000 cavalrymen out of Salem, Virginia, on his brave but foolish ride. Within two days, Stuart's plan fell apart. Every time he tried to get around the head of the Union army, he found long lines of marching infantry blocking his way. The seven corps of the Army of the Potomac—each a little more than half the size of a Confederate corps—were marching north faster than Lee or Stuart had expected. But try as he might, Stuart could not get this vital news through to his chief. Meanwhile, stripped of his cavalry, Lee marched blindly across the narrow handle of Maryland and into Pennsylvania.

On June 26, Lee established his headquarters in Chambersburg, Pennsylvania. While Lee waited for Longstreet's and A. P. Hill's corps to come up from the south, Ewell pushed on toward the Pennsylva-

*At the end of a long day's march, Union soldiers
relax on a hill overlooking their camp.*

nia state capital of Harrisburg on the Susquehanna
River. To better sweep the area for supplies, Ewell's
corps advanced along two roads. General Jubal
Early's division took the southeasterly route, brush-
ing off some Pennsylvania militia (state troops with
little training) before marching through a sleepy
town called Gettysburg. About the only thing re-
markable about this town of some two thousand was

its position at the hub of nine roads. Early's men paused long enough to buy everything in the local stores with Confederate money that had almost no value in the North, then continued their march across the rolling Pennsylvania farmland.

Back in Chambersburg, Lee was growing increasingly worried. Where was Stuart and where was the Union army? No one had any good answers. On the night of June 28, a spy in Longstreet's pay arrived with stunning news. The Union army had crossed the Potomac two days before and was pushing hard through Maryland toward Pennsylvania. "Fighting Joe" Hooker was no longer in command; Lincoln had replaced him with General George Gordon Meade.

Lee knew that "Old Snapping Turtle" Meade would be a far more dangerous opponent than Hooker. Unless the Confederates moved quickly, Meade might destroy Lee's widely separated corps one by one. Lee studied his maps and decided to use the web of roads around Gettysburg to bring his army together. He sent a message recalling Ewell from the north and set Hill's corps marching east with instructions to camp a few miles west of Gettysburg to wait for Ewell. Lee would follow with Longstreet's corps. One of Lee's aides suggested that Meade would prove no better than Hooker. But

Lee disagreed: "General Meade will make no blunder on my front."

George Gordon Meade had not expected to command the Army of the Potomac. Forty-eight but looking much older, he had spent most of his career as a military engineer. With few flashy assignments to his credit and a reputation for fits of temper, he made few friends in high places. But Lincoln noticed that even when Lee was thrashing the Union army, Meade's men always seemed to do better than the rest. Perhaps in Meade he had finally found the fighter the Army of the Potomac needed. With the most important battle of the war perhaps only days away, Lincoln fired Hooker and appointed Meade.

Meade pushed north fast, determined to find Lee. As the Union army crossed into Pennsylvania, Meade studied the land. If he could find a good defensive position, he would halt the army and try to lure Lee into attacking. At Pipe Creek, a dozen miles south of Gettysburg, Meade spotted ground to his liking. By this time the Army of the Potomac was spread out in a huge arc twenty-five miles wide. Like Lee, Meade needed to pull his army together before risking battle. He began writing orders. But a hard-driving Union cavalry officer named Buford and the Confederate lack of shoes would change both commanders' plans.

Major General George Gordon Meade, commander of the Union Army of the Potomac. Only days before Gettysburg, the grim, hot-tempered Meade became the army's fourth commander in less than two years.

General John Buford led 4,000 Union cavalry into Gettysburg on the morning of June 30. As the lead troops trotted through town, a brigade of Confederate infantry came down the Chambersburg Pike from the west, hesitated, then pulled back. Buford didn't know who they were for sure, but he sensed power behind those few regiments. He had fought Indians before the war and had long ago learned to trust his sense of danger. He posted one of his brigades along McPherson's Ridge a mile west of Gettysburg, positioned the other north of town, then sent a report to his commander, General John Reynolds.

Buford established his headquarters for the night in the Lutheran college on Seminary Ridge, midway between Gettysburg and McPherson's Ridge. That evening one of the Union officers bragged that he would easily handle anything that the Confederates threw at him. Buford shook his head. "No, you won't. They will attack in the morning and they will come booming. . . . You will have to fight like the devil."

The Confederate troops Buford had seen that afternoon belonged to General Henry Heth's division of A. P. Hill's corps. That night, Heth visited Hill's headquarters a few miles west of Gettysburg. Heth had heard talk of a vast supply of shoes hidden in Gettysburg. There were reports of a few blue-clad soldiers in the vicinity—probably Pennsylvania militia—but nothing much to worry about. Would Hill have any objection if Heth took his division and went after the shoes? "None in the world," Hill replied.

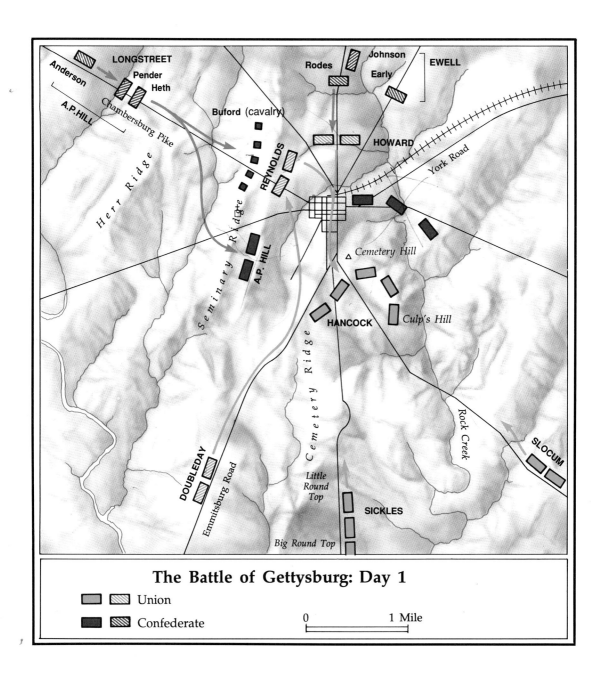

Anderson

A.P. HILL

LONGSTREET

Pender

Heth

Chambersburg Pike

Herr Ridge

Buford (cavalry)

REYNOLDS

Seminary Ridge

A.P. HILL

DOUBLEDAY

Emmitsburg Road

Rodes

Johnson

Early

EWELL

HOWARD

York Road

Cemetery Hill

HANCOCK

Culp's Hill

Cemetery Ridge

Little
Round
Top

Rock Creek

SLOCUM

SICKLES

Big Round Top

The Battle of Gettysburg: Day 1

Union

Confederate

0   1 Mile

2

THE DEVIL TO PAY

Heth's Confederates came booming down the Chambersburg Pike at eight o'clock on the morning of July 1, 1863. Buford's men were waiting on McPherson's Ridge a mile west of Gettysburg. Although outnumbered two to one, the Union cavalry had a nasty surprise waiting for the Southerners—the Spencer breech-loading carbine.

The vast majority of Civil War rifles were muzzle-loaders. A soldier had to go through nine steps to load and fire a single shot. A veteran might fire four shots a minute, but Buford's men could get off seven shots in the same time with a Spencer.

The rapid fire of Buford's men halted the Confederate advance. Heth brought up a dozen cannons and threw in reinforcements. The fight grew hotter.

Bristling with weapons, this glowering Union soldier poses in a photographer's studio. In actual battle, he would have put sword and dagger aside and depended on his muzzle-loading rifle, with its detachable knife called a bayonet.

In the tower of the Lutheran Seminary, Buford watched through binoculars. He knew that his men couldn't hold much longer against the growing Confederate numbers. A calm voice spoke behind him. "What's the matter, John?"

Buford turned to see General John Reynolds, probably the best-liked and most respected general in the army. "There's the devil to pay," Buford replied.

Could his men hold for an hour? Reynolds asked. Buford thought so. Reynolds hurried to his horse and galloped down the road to the south where Union infantry were approaching at a trot. He guided the lead division across country to McPherson's Ridge. If he could get them there in time, he might yet beat the Confederates back. Ahead an apple orchard swarmed with Confederates. Reynolds waved his men on, crying, "Forward. For God's sake, forward!" Just then, a Confederate bullet slammed into his brain.

The Union infantry swept by their dying general and went roaring into the battle. The famed Iron Brigade of tough Wisconsin, Michigan, and Indiana veterans hit the right end, or flank, of the Confederate line. On seeing the black hats of the Iron Brigade, one Confederate yelled, "That ain't no militia. That's the Army of the Potomac!"

The two great armies had collided almost by accident. Neither army commander was ready for battle and both were still miles from the scene. But generals' plans mattered little to the thousands of soldiers fighting desperately in the fields and woods west of Gettysburg. South of the Chambersburg Pike, the fierce Union counterattack forced the Confederates back. To the north of the pike, the situation was reversed, as Mississippi and North Carolina troops drove the Northerners toward Seminary Ridge. General Abner Doubleday, now the senior Union commander, hurled his infantry reserve into the fight, stopping the Confederate attack cold.

After three hours of heavy fighting, both sides paused for breath. It was 11:00 A.M. and already the dead, wounded, and captured numbered in the thousands.

General Oliver O. Howard brought his XI Corps into Gettysburg at noon and took overall command from Doubleday. He put his men into line to the right of Doubleday's as Buford's exhausted cavalry pulled back. The cannons of the two armies blazed away. Suddenly a shell howled over the Union line from a different direction. To the north a new Confederate battery of guns was in action. Behind it long columns of butternut-clad infantry came hurrying down the road. Marching to rejoin Lee, "Baldy" Ewell's corps had stumbled into the fight at Gettysburg.

Howard moved quickly, swinging back the northern end of his line and ordering two freshly arrived divisions into a new line north of Gettysburg. They barely had time to find cover before Ewell's men attacked. The commander of Ewell's lead division, General Robert Rodes, failed to scout the land in front of him, and his men paid heavily for the mistake. Howard's men hid behind walls and trees and cut them down by the hundreds.

At this point, Lee rode through Heth's battered division. He received Heth's report, then raised his binoculars to study the scene to the north where Rodes was taking a pounding. Heth begged for permission to attack again. Lee refused: No, the army wasn't ready for a major battle. He was about to order a retreat when two stunning blows changed the course of the fight. One of Rodes's brigades hit the gap between the Union lines on the north and the west. At almost the same moment, Jubal Early's division came whooping down the road from the northwest to smash into the far right end of the Union line. Howard's men broke formation and ran.

Lee changed his mind instantly. A. P. Hill had just ridden up, and Lee ordered him to strike hard at Doubleday's Union corps in front of them. Joined by another division, Heth's men charged across the ground already bloody with the morning's fighting. They took and gave terrible punishment. Entire regiments disappeared in the fighting. The 24th Michigan lost 399 of 496 men, the attacking 26th North Carolina even more. But with the Union line to the north broken, Doubleday's men had to give way. They retreated slowly up Seminary Ridge, then broke and joined the rush into Gettysburg.

Howard had positioned a reserve division in Gettysburg's hilltop cemetery a half mile south of town. Seeing their fleeing comrades, the Union troops on Cemetery Hill frantically started digging defensive positions. They were joined by some of the retreating soldiers, but thousands of Union troops were captured in the streets of Gettysburg and thousands more just kept running. On Cemetery Hill, Howard stood waving his sword, hopelessly trying to stop the rout.

At that moment of nearly complete disaster, a new general rode onto Cemetery Hill. Meade had sent Winfield Scott Hancock to take command. The tall, handsome Hancock was one of the Union army's most respected leaders. The soldiers saw him and redoubled their efforts. Hancock took a quick look at the battlefield and knew what he had to do.

The ridge south of Gettysburg is shaped rather like a fishhook. At its southern end, the eye of the fishhook is formed by a high hill called Big Round Top. To its north is a lower hill called Little Round

Top. Cemetery Ridge forms the shaft of the fishhook as it rises from swampy ground at the foot of Little Round Top to the crest of Cemetery Hill. The ridge then curves east, dropping into a saddle, then rising again until it reaches Culp's Hill at the barb of the hook. Hancock saw that the ridge was a defensive position of great natural strength. Somehow he had to keep it in Union hands.

Since early morning both sides had been pouring men into the battle until the Union defenders numbered about 20,000 against 25,000 Confederate attackers. Lee's army had lost some 8,000 men, but still had about 17,000 fit for duty and more on the way. The Union defenders were in far worse shape. About 9,000 Union soldiers were dead, wounded, or captured, and another 5,000 had scattered, leaving Hancock only 6,000 men to hold the ridge.

A lesser general would have ordered a retreat. Hancock did not. He ordered Doubleday to send a division to Culp's Hill, then strung the rest of the Union soldiers in a thin line from Cemetery Hill along the ridge toward Little Round Top. He sent messengers dashing down the road with pleas for more men. Every minute counted now. Hancock stared across the shallow valley toward Seminary Ridge less than a mile away and wondered how much time the Confederates would give him.

TOOLS OF THE ARMIES

A Union battle flag.

Lee's ill-shod Confederates came to Gettysburg looking for shoes.

In the heat of battle, a full canteen was precious.

ALABAMA

On Seminary Ridge, Lee was also studying the land. If the Confederates could take Cemetery Ridge, Meade would have to attack on Lee's terms. Lee asked Hill if his corps could attack again. Hill said no, his men were just too beat up from the long day's fighting. Lee sent a message to Ewell, suggesting that he attack if he thought he could "push those people from the hill."

Unsure of himself, Ewell hesitated. Precious minutes slipped by. On Cemetery Ridge, Hancock's men dug furiously. Another Union corps began arriving. Still Ewell delayed. Daylight began to fade and with it the Confederate hopes. Longstreet joined Lee on Seminary Ridge and suggested that the army find better ground and wait for Meade to attack, but Lee refused to give up the idea of taking the fight to the enemy.

By nightfall, Hancock had added two fresh corps to a line stretching the three miles from Little Round Top to Culp's Hill. He turned over command to another general and rode south to Meade's headquarters at Taneytown. Hancock found that Meade had already decided to "order up the troops." Both armies were now committed to the greatest battle in the history of North America.

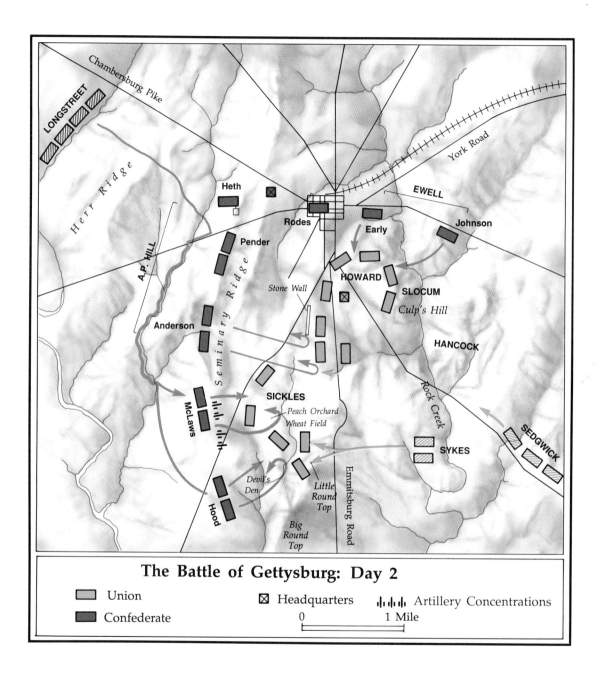

Chambersburg Pike

LONGSTREET

Herr Ridge

A.P. HILL

Heth

Pender

Rodes

Stone Wall

Anderson

Seminary Ridge

McLaws

SICKLES

Peach Orchard

Wheat Field

Devil's Den

Hood

York Road

EWELL

Early

Johnson

HOWARD

SLOCUM

Culp's Hill

HANCOCK

Rock Creek

Little Round Top

Big Round Top

Emmitsburg Road

SYKES

SEDGWICK

The Battle of Gettysburg: Day 2

Union

Confederate

⊠ Headquarters

╷╷╷╷╷ Artillery Concentrations

0   1 Mile

3
LIKE DEMONS FROM THE EARTH

General Meade rode onto Cemetery Ridge at 3:00 A.M. on July 2. Three of his generals greeted him with the news that the army held an excellent defensive position. Meade replied, "I am glad to hear you say so, gentlemen, for it is too late to leave it."

By dawn, Meade had six of his seven corps in place along the curving line from Culp's Hill to Little Round Top. It was indeed an excellent position. Meade could rush reinforcements to any threatened point in a matter of minutes. When General John Sedgwick brought his VI Corps puffing onto the field that afternoon after a blistering thirty-two-mile march, Meade would have some 80,000 men and 354 cannons.

Cannons were critical to Meade's defense. The

standard Civil War cannon was the smooth-bore "Napoleon." It could fire twelve-pound solid balls, hollow shells filled with gunpowder, or deadly rounds of canister—tin cans packed with small lead balls. Between shots, the crew cleaned the barrel with a swab—a wet sponge on a long handle—to put out any sparks that could touch off the next round of gunpowder. A good gun crew could fire three or four rounds per minute, and Meade's gunners were among the best in the world.

After the heavy losses on July 1, Lee had about 50,000 men and 272 cannons. Although outnumbered, Lee had the advantage of choosing when and where to attack. He decided to send Longstreet's First Corps against the Union left. As the attack rolled north, Hill would throw in Third Corps. Meanwhile, Ewell would attack the far right of the Union line with his Second Corps, pinning down the defenders and keeping Meade from reinforcing other parts of his line.

Longstreet still disagreed with Lee, preferring to defend rather than attack, but he followed orders. He worked his two divisions into position, hiding their movement behind Seminary Ridge.

The day grew hot as noon passed. The Union troops waited nervously along the ridge. The 10,000 men of General Dan Sickles's III Corps occupied the far left of the Union line where Cemetery Ridge dipped into swampy ground north of Little Round Top. Sickles did not like his position. A half mile into the valley, a peach orchard stood on a low hill. Sickles asked permission to move his corps forward to this higher ground. He was turned down, but the stubborn Sickles chose to misunderstand.

Sickles was not a professional soldier but a politician from New York City who had used political ties to get his rank. His lack of experience and good judgment would nearly lose the battle. Shortly after noon, III Corps, flags flying and bands playing, marched into the valley to the peach orchard and the nearby wheat field. Watching from Cemetery Ridge, General Hancock was astonished by the stupidity of the move. Sickles had created a bulge in the Union line that could be attacked from three sides. Even worse, Sickles had opened a half-mile gap between III Corps and Hancock's II Corps.

At 3:00 P.M., Longstreet's cannons began a tremendous bombardment of the Union line. Lee's plan called for an attack up the Emmitsburg road "in echelon." This meant that the farthest right-hand brigade of the southernmost division would attack first, followed by the one to its left and so on—brigade after brigade, division after division, building to a tremendous rolling wave.

Neither of Longstreet's division commanders liked the plan. General John Bell Hood, commander of the southernmost division, begged for permission to sweep around the Round Tops to attack the Union rear. Longstreet replied, "We must obey the orders of General Lee."

General Meade heard the roar of the Confederate cannons and rushed to the southern end of his line accompanied by his chief engineer, General Gouverneur Warren. They were shocked to find Sickles's assigned position empty. Warren swung away to climb Little Round Top while Meade galloped to the peach orchard. When he found Sickles, Old Snapping Turtle held his temper: "General, I am afraid you are out too far." Sickles, still disagreeing, offered to pull back. Meade shook his head. "I think it is too late. The enemy will not allow you."

As Meade spurred to the rear for reinforcements, Warren reached the crest of Little Round Top. Another nasty shock awaited him. The day before, Hancock had sent troops to take control of the hill overlooking Cemetery Ridge. Hancock had seen—as any good general would—that Little Round Top was the key to the Union defense. Farther south, tree-covered Big Round Top was of little importance, but a few enemy cannons on treeless Little Round Top could pound the length of the Union line. When

Hancock's men had moved to new positions, the defense of Little Round Top had been left to Sickles's corps. And Sickles had done nothing! A horrified Warren found the top of the hill unmanned except for a few Union signalmen. He sent an aide scurrying down the rocky slope to find troops.

Warren had only minutes to save Little Round Top. At 4:00 P.M., Hood opened the Confederate infantry attack. Instead of advancing up the Emmitsburg road as ordered, his first brigade charged straight toward the ridge and the far end of Sickles's line. Sickles's men waited in a jumble of boulders called the Devil's Den. The Confederates came on, giving their high rebel yells. A Union officer would recall that they sounded "like demons emerging from the earth."

In minutes, the Devil's Den became a true hell. Hundreds of men scrambled among the rocks, shooting, clubbing, and slashing at each other until blood stood in pools. Several of Hood's regiments under Colonel William Oates swept around the Devil's Den, drove some snipers from the wooded slope of Big Round Top, and charged up Little Round Top. Union troops coming from the other side beat them by minutes. A frantic struggle raged along the crest of the hill. Warren brought another Union brigade scrambling up the hill. Union gunners wrestled six cannons over rocks and brush to the top. They opened fire using double loads of canister, spraying the Confederates with death.

On the south slope of Little Round Top, the 20th Maine regiment held the farthest point of the Union line. If the Maine regiment cracked, so would the entire Union defense of Little Round Top. With Little Round Top would go the whole Union line, the battle, and perhaps the future of the Union. As a nation's fate hung in the balance, the 20th Maine held against five charges by the 15th Alabama. Bleeding, bruised, and nearly out of ammunition, the Maine soldiers then did the unbelievable: they fixed bayonets to their rifles and charged. The Southern attack broke. The Confederates retreated to the Devil's Den, where the rest of Hood's men had finally overpowered Sickles's troops. The Union gunners fired round after round after them. Bursting cannonballs sent iron fragments shrieking among the rocks to mix with the screams of wounded and dying men.

North of the Devil's Den, General Lafayette McLaws's division slammed into Sickles's line at the wheat field. Meade threw a full division in to reinforce III Corps. Hancock pulled two brigades out of II Corps's line and sent them to Sickles's aid. The men of the Irish Brigade, made up of recent immi-

In desperate fighting on July 2, Union soldiers held Little Round Top—the key to the Northern line—against repeated charges by Confederate troops.

*Father William Corby blessed the Irish Brigade
before it charged into the bloody fight in the
wheat field on the second day of battle.*

grants, knelt while a priest climbed a rock and blessed them. Then they charged into the horror. Union soldiers splashing across Plum Run, the stream flowing past the wheat field, saw its waters turned red with blood. The fight raged back and forth across what one soldier would call "the terrible, terrible wheat field"—the bloodiest ground of a bloody war.

Another Confederate brigade smashed through Sickles's line at the peach orchard. Led by General William Barksdale—his long white hair streaming— the Mississippians captured a thousand of Sickles's men in a swoop and drove the rest toward Cemetery Ridge. This wasn't enough for Barksdale. He waved his sword forward and led his cheering men in a charge for the heights. Union gunners fired double loads of canister down on them. A Union officer assigned a full company to aim at Barksdale: "That big Reb. Get him." Barksdale fell with five bullets in his body, and Union rifle and cannon fire smothered the attack.

North of the peach orchard, General Richard Anderson's division of Hill's corps joined the attack. An Alabama brigade hit the gap left by Sickles between III and II Corps and came roaring up the ridge unopposed. Hancock saw them coming. He had already sent his reserves to Sickles and had nothing left to stop the charging Alabamans. In desperation, he ordered his farthest right-hand division to abandon its position and come at the run. The gamble might work if he could somehow slow the Confederates: "I saw that five minutes must be gained or we were lost."

Hancock galloped to the crest of the ridge, bullets whizzing around him. He found the first troops hurrying to plug the gap. "What regiment is this?" he shouted. "First Minnesota," came the reply. Hancock pointed to the Confederates' flag: "Do you see those colors? Take them." After many battles, the 1st Minnesota had only 262 men left, but they fixed bayonets and charged the vastly larger Confederate brigade. The astounded Alabamans staggered, then regained their footing, and crushed the Minnesotans. Only forty-seven men of the 1st Minnesota made it back, but they had given Hancock not five but a full ten minutes to plug the hole in the Union line. Blasts from massed Union cannons and rifles swept the Alabamans off the ridge.

Four hundred yards farther north, a Georgia brigade overran Hancock's weakened line. For a moment, Confederate battle flags waved atop Cemetery Ridge in the late afternoon sun. Then General Meade hit the Southerners with a counterattack that threw them back into the valley. The great Confederate attack shuddered to a halt.

All through the struggle, Ewell had done almost nothing against the Union right. In the dusk, he finally attacked. The Union line was weak, most of its defenders long since sent to fight at the other end of the ridge. Ewell's left-hand division stormed up Culp's Hill but ran into a seasoned brigade of New Yorkers and what was left of the once mighty Iron

Brigade. The tough Union veterans stopped the Confederates cold. To the west, two brigades of Jubal Early's division punched through three lines manned by General Howard's unlucky XI Corps to reach the top of Cemetery Hill. Hancock again saved the day by hurling a brigade into the hole. Howard's men rallied and charged back into the fight, driving the Confederates down the hill in the dark.

Night fell over Gettysburg. Along the slopes of Cemetery Ridge and far out into the valley, the dead and the dying lay in the cold light of the moon. Men so tired that they could no longer feel slept while the wounded cried for help, water, or a mother, wife, or sweetheart far away. Some ten thousand men on each side had fallen on July 2, making Gettysburg the bloodiest battle of a tragic war.

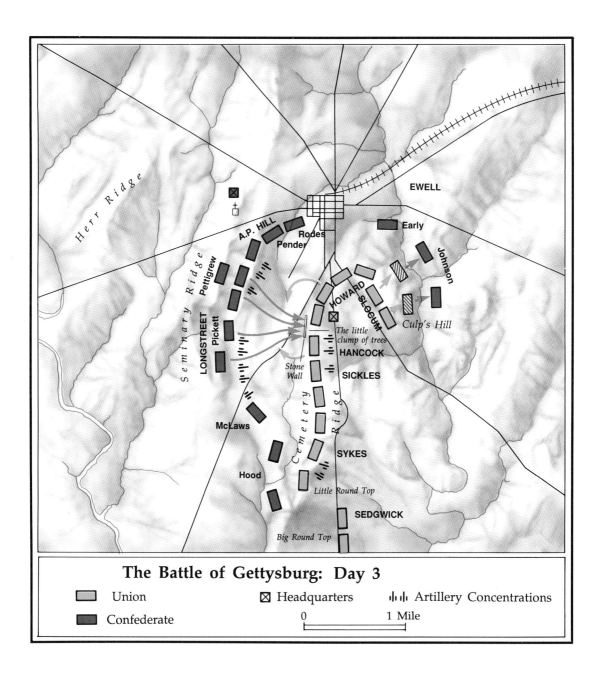

Herr Ridge

EWELL

A.P. HILL

Rodes
Pender

Early

Johnson

Seminary Ridge
Pettigrew

HOWARD

SLOCUM

Culp's Hill

LONGSTREET
Pickett

The little
clump of trees

HANCOCK

Stone
Wall

SICKLES

McLaws

Cemetery Ridge

SYKES

Hood

Little Round Top

SEDGWICK

Big Round Top

The Battle of Gettysburg: Day 3

Union   ⊠ Headquarters   ᏒᏒ Artillery Concentrations

Confederate

0   1 Mile

4

THE TIDE TURNED BACK

Robert E. Lee had become a very stubborn man. He had tried to break both ends of the Union line and very nearly succeeded. Now he would try the center.

By midnight of July 2, Lee had made his plans. Ewell would attack the Union right at dawn, capturing Culp's Hill and pinning down a good part of Meade's army. Meanwhile, Lee would line up every cannon he could find for a tremendous shelling of the Union line south of Cemetery Hill. Longstreet's and Hill's infantry would smash through the weakened line and scatter Meade's army. Jeb Stuart, who had finally arrived late that afternoon with his exhausted Confederate cavalry, would fall on the retreating troops to complete the destruction of the Army of the Potomac.

Lee explained the plan to Longstreet shortly after sunrise on July 3. Longstreet was horrified. His infantry would have to attack across nearly a mile of open ground under the fire of scores of Union cannons and thousands of rifles. He begged Lee to reconsider. The army should slide around the Union left to get between Gettysburg and Washington. Then Meade would have to attack on Lee's terms. But Lee shook his fist at Cemetery Ridge: "The enemy is there, and I am going to strike him."

Longstreet knew that further argument was pointless. Together, the two generals rode along Seminary Ridge to inspect the army. Already, they could hear the sounds of battle to the north around Culp's Hill. Meade had not waited for Ewell to attack. Union cannons on Culp's Hill had begun firing at 3:45 A.M., opening nearly seven hours of fighting. Union and Confederate troops fought back and forth through the woods in savage attacks and counterattacks. The greater number of Union cannons made the difference. By late morning, Ewell's troops were driven off the slopes.

The failure did not change Lee's plan. He watched Colonel E. Porter Alexander, Longstreet's artillery chief, bring battery after battery of cannons into a two-mile arc facing Cemetery Ridge. Lee turned away to visit General George Pickett, whose division would form the core of the infantry attack.

Pickett had never been so happy. His men had missed the first two days of fighting, but now they would have their chance for glory. Pickett was thirty-eight, a dashing, handsome man with "perfumed ringlets" falling to his shoulders. No one in the army thought he was very smart, but he was very brave—brave enough to take his men straight into the teeth of the Union guns on Cemetery Ridge.

Lee gave Pickett two of Hill's brigades to go along with his three. To the north, General James Johnston Pettigrew would lead four more of Hill's brigades with two more following close behind. In all, eleven brigades numbering some 12,500 men would attack the Union center.

Unlike Pickett's fresh division, most of Hill's brigades had suffered heavily in the first two days. As he rode along, Lee was shocked to see the number of walking wounded in the thin ranks. He spoke softly, "Many of these poor boys should be in the rear." Then grimly, "The attack must succeed."

The day grew hot as noon approached. In the valley, there was a sharp fight over a farmhouse and barn. Union troops set them afire and retreated. As the column of smoke rose lazily into the hot blue sky, an unearthly quiet fell over the battlefield. On both sides, men whispered and walked on tiptoe.

At 1:07 P.M., the report of a signal gun shattered the quiet. With a roar, 175 Confederate cannons opened the greatest bombardment in the history of the continent. About 120 Union cannons answered. Civilians in Washington, sixty miles away, heard distant thunder and wondered what storm was about to break.

A whirlwind of screaming iron hit the center of the Union line. The Northern soldiers dove for cover. As one said, "It seemed nothing four feet above the ground could live." Shells exploded overhead, solid cannonballs smashed into stone, earth, and flesh. Caissons carrying ammunition for the Union guns disappeared in deafening blasts as the fire struck home. Cannonballs slammed into General Meade's headquarters in a cottage a few hundred feet to the rear. Sixteen horses in the yard were killed, and splinters nearly hit Meade himself. The general and his staff had to retreat to safer ground.

Smoke filled the valley between the lines. Unable to make out their targets, the Confederate gunners started shooting long, most of their shells passing over the troops on Cemetery Ridge and landing among the wagons and supplies in the Union rear. General Hancock rode calmly along his line, ignoring the cannonballs and fragments whizzing past. His men cheered.

The 5,700 men of Hancock's II Corps held the center of the Union line along a low stone wall. Near its middle, the wall jogged to the west for eighty yards to avoid a small grove of trees, then turned back to the south. Hancock did not know it yet, but Lee had ordered Pickett to head for that grove at the angle in the stone wall.

Out in front of the Confederate guns, Colonel Alexander was trying to determine if the furious fire was driving the Union cannons from the ridge. After an hour and a half, ammunition was running short; if the infantry were to attack, it would have to be soon. The Union fire seemed to lessen. The eighteen guns he'd counted in the grove fell silent. He sent a note to Pickett: "For God's sake, come quick."

Pickett was standing near where Longstreet sat on a rail fence. "General, shall I advance?" Old Pete could not trust himself to speak but only nodded.

The Confederate guns fell silent, and another eerie quiet fell over the valley. Through the smoke, the sun glowed blood red. Slowly the smoke drifted away, and the Union troops on Cemetery Ridge saw a sight they would never forget. A mile-long line of butternut-clad infantrymen emerged from the haze, marching steadily across the green fields. For three minutes, they came on like an unstoppable tide. Then the Union cannons opened fire.

Alexander had been wrong. General Henry Hunt, Meade's artillery commander, had tricked him by ordering the Union guns to cease fire. Plenty remained on the ridge and Hunt was bringing up more. The Union gunners found the range. Fire from Cemetery Hill and Little Round Top cut cruelly at the flanks of the Confederate line. Hancock's guns blazed at them from dead ahead. Scores, then hundreds of Confederates were swept away, but the ranks closed and came on toward the ridge.

A quarter-mile opening lay between Pickett's men on the south and Pettigrew's on the north. Pickett gave the order "left oblique" and his men moved at a diagonal to the left. It took added time, and all the while the shells from the heights slashed at them. Halfway across the valley, Pickett ordered a halt. On the heights, an awed Union soldier cried, "My God, they're dressing the line!" As if on a parade ground, the Confederates sidestepped to close the line. The sweating Union gunners fired, swabbed, loaded, and fired again. The Confederate line shrank, pulling in tighter as the Union cannon fire slammed home. Finally, Pickett gave the order to resume the march.

Two hundred yards short of the Emmitsburg road, a regiment of Union infantry sprang from cover and poured a deadly volley into Pettigrew's left flank. Four Confederate regiments broke and ran, but the rest marched on. From behind the fences along the road, another Union regiment rose up and delivered a frightening volley before racing for the cover of the ridge 400 yards behind.

The Confederates charged, surging across the road in a wave 500 yards wide. Blasts of Union canister tore "wagon-wide swaths" in the Confederate ranks as they swept up the slope toward the stone wall. A sheet of rifle fire hit them as Hancock's men fired. But still the Confederates came on, shooting, yelling, and believing yet in the impossible.

General Lewis Armistead, his black hat atop his sword, led them toward the angle in the wall. On the far side, Lieutenant Alonzo Cushing, a young Union artillery officer, yelled, "Triple canister, no swab!" A bullet hit him in the mouth, dropping him dead. His gunners fired their last terrible load, as the Union infantry broke. Armistead leaped the wall, his men pouring after him.

To the north, the Union line swung out like a gate to fire on the Confederate left flank. Hancock dashed down the line to order his men on the south to do the same. Near the angle, Colonel Arthur Devereux, commanding two reserve regiments, yelled to him and pointed toward the Confederates seething over the wall. "Get in there!" Hancock shouted. As Hancock's men on the left swept out to blast the Confederate right flank, Devereux's regiments hit the Southerners head on. Armistead fell mortally wounded, his hand reaching for Cushing's cannon. Fired on from three sides, the Confederate attack staggered to a halt. For a few desperate min-

Above: Pickett's Charge on July 3 nearly overran the Union center, but the "High Tide of the Confederacy" broke a few yards short of the crest of Cemetery Ridge. Opposite: In the final assault, Confederates capture a Union cannon at the angle.

utes, the fight swirled around the angle, then slowly, stubbornly, the Confederates gave way.

The high tide of the Confederacy broke a few yards short of the crest of Cemetery Ridge. The last wave fell back across the valley, leaving behind broken men and the shattered dream of Southern victory. General Lee rode among the bleeding, dazed survivors. "This is all my fault," he told them. "Now you must help me."

What history would call Pickett's Charge marked the end of the major fighting at Gettysburg. Lee organized a defense, while Hancock—wounded in the final minutes of the battle—begged Meade to attack. But Meade was cautious. His army had taken terrible punishment, too. "We have done well enough," he said.

Through July 4, the eighty-seventh anniversary of the nation's birth, the two armies lay exhausted. That night, in a heavy rain, the Army of Northern Virginia began its long retreat home. The Army of the Potomac followed but did not attack until it was too late to prevent Lee's escape across the Potomac.

On the fields of Gettysburg, the suffering went on. Exhausted doctors could give only the crudest treatment to the thousands of wounded. Civilian volunteers came by the hundreds to help. But for many soldiers, no hope remained.

Confederate losses in dead, wounded, and cap-

*The dead littered the fields of Gettysburg in the
bloodiest battle in the history of North America.*

THE GENERALS AND THEIR FATES

Dan Sickles
(1819–1914)
Politician

Winfield S. Hancock
(1824–86)
Presidential candidate 1880

John Buford
(1826–63)
Died of exhaustion

Joseph "Fighting Joe" Hooker
(1814–79)
Retired in 1868

Abner Doubleday
(1819–93)
"Inventor" of baseball

John Sedgwick
(1813–64)
Killed at Spotsylvania

A. P. Hill
(1825–65)
Killed at Petersburg, Va.

Richard Ewell
(1817–72)
Retired because of wounds

James Longstreet
(1821–1904)
Federal official

Jubal Early
(1816–94)
Lawyer

George Pickett
(1825–75)
Businessman

J. E. B. Stuart
(1833–64)
Killed at Yellow Tavern

tured numbered some 28,000 at Gettysburg, more than a third of Lee's army. Meade lost some 23,000, a quarter of his army. But the North could replace its losses, while the life blood of the South was bleeding away. On the same day Lee began his retreat, Vicksburg surrendered to General Ulysses S. Grant. Lincoln would bring Grant east the next year. At a terrible cost, Grant would finally hammer the South into surrender.

On a mild fall day in November 1863, with victory still a year and a half away, Abraham Lincoln came to Gettysburg to dedicate a cemetery for the fallen. He sat through a flowery two-hour speech by Edward Everett, the greatest orator of the age. At last, it was the president's turn. Tall and gaunt, he moved to the front. His voice was high, and many in the restless audience had difficulty hearing his words. His speech lasted only three minutes, and even Lincoln thought it was a failure.

Today, hardly an American has not heard of Lincoln's Gettysburg Address. More prayer than speech, its words reach across the generations from that distant battlefield. It calls on us even now to ensure that those who "gave the last full measure of devotion . . . shall not have died in vain—that this nation, under God, shall have a new birth of freedom— and that government of the people, by the people, for the people, shall not perish from the earth."

Gettysburg National Memorial Park today.
The North Carolina Monument (inset) freezes
a desperate moment in Pickett's Charge.

SUGGESTED READING

Carter, Hodding. *Robert E. Lee and the Road of Honor.* New York: Random House, 1955.

Catton, Bruce. *The Battle of Gettysburg.* New York: American Heritage, 1963.

Clark, Champ. *Gettysburg: The Confederate High Tide.* Alexandria, Va.: Time-Life Books, 1985.

Jordan, Robert Paul. *The Civil War.* Washington, D.C.: National Geographic, 1969.

Kantor, MacKinlay. *Gettysburg.* New York: Random House, 1952.

Phelan, Mary Kay. *Mr. Lincoln Speaks at Gettysburg.* New York: W. W. Norton, 1966.

Weidborn, Manfred. *Robert E. Lee.* New York: Atheneum, 1988.

Windrow, Martin. *The Civil War Rifleman.* New York: Franklin Watts, 1985.

INDEX